THE THOUGHTS AND FEELINGS OF A LONELY WOLF

Akean O'malley Jr
The thoughts and Feelings of a Lonely Wolf

Published by Spines
ISBN: 979-8-89383-064-4

THE THOUGHTS AND FEELINGS OF A LONELY WOLF

AKEAN O'MALLEY JR

DEDICATION

I want to dedicate this book to both of my grandmothers for always pushing me to achieve my dreams, and to my moms for their love and support.

ACKNOWLEDGMENTS

I want to thank all the people that inspire me to express myself in a creative way, like Kaydiana O'Malley, Kidara O'Malley, Kelsey O'Malley, Francie Lentini, B.J Washington, Victor Butler, Raymond Adamkiewicz, Laurie Harriton, Matt Brown, Emily Crocker, Sonia Prass, Kathleen Lamb, David Zodda, Alexander Yarde, Elzabeth Wilkins, Carman Shell, Sherry Shcks, Ebony Omelagan.

TABLE OF CONTENTS

<u>A Better Place</u>

One Panamanian

One Jamaican

One Asian

One American

One from every race

One from every faith

To make the world a better place for you and me.

<u>A Nation United</u>

After September 11th occurred
It left us in a state of mourning

It left us in a state of grief

A state that can't be expressed by words
Only my tears

It left many in a state of loneliness

But out of all this disaster
We stood together as one

We helped and look out for each other

We remain as one nation that can't be broken

If we stand for justice, liberty and freedom for all people
And all nationalities
Then we will be a nation that truly stands for
Liberty &Justice
For all mankind.

A Toast To The Times

A toast to the time we first met each other
To the time we became more then friends
To the time we fell in love
To the time we move in together
To the time nothing could break us apart
To the good times & the bad
To the time of us getting old together
To the times we share.

<u>Ain't I The One</u>

Ain't I the one who let you in?

The one who love you

The one who did anything for you

The one who treat you like queen

The one who gave you everything I had

The one who was there

When you need someone to talk to

Someone to turn to

Someone to count on

The one who always stood by your side

For you to turn against me

And leave me for another guy.

<u>All I Want</u>

All I want is to be free

From the lies

From the cheating ways

From being lonely

From the Games they play

From the heart aches

From the false commitments

I just want to be free from ever falling in love again.

<u>Am I In Love?</u>

Am I in love with you?

Have I finally found that special one?

That was made for me

The one I always dream of

The one that brings joy to my painful soul

The one that sees past my shortcomings

The one that makes me a better man

The one that shows me how true love feels

The one I want to spend the rest my life with.

<u>As The Sun Rises</u>

As the sun rise and set

A new life is giving to the world

But as some was giving

Some was taking and the world have lost

The next Marcus Garvey

The next Madam CJ Walker

The next Booker T Washington

The next Thurgood Marshall

The next George Washington Carver

Who to say the next president of the free world?

<u>Being With You</u>

Being with you has brightened my days

Being with you has given me hope I never had

Being with you has made me a better man

Being with you has made me whole

Being with you I don't feel lost and alone

Being with you has taken away all my misery and sorrow

Being with you has answered all my prays

And I thank The Most High for you.

<u>Black Liberty</u>

Black liberty that stands for freedom

Black liberty that stand for justice

Black liberty that Stand for life

Black liberty that stand for hope

Black liberty that stands for braver

Black liberty that stand for peace

Black liberty that stand for love

Black liberty that stands for you and me.

Can I

Can I trust you with my deepest secrets?

Can I be myself around you?

Can I turn to you for advice?

Can I give you my heart?

Can I know that you will always be by my side?

Can I believe that what we have is more than a thing but true love?

Can I?

<u>Can You</u>

Can you give me some time to?
Show you that I'm not the same person you knew

That I have changed my ways

To just be with you

That I realize that I'm nothing without you

That you are all that I needed

That you are the only one made for me

The only one that could see through my bull shit

The only love that is my anchor

The only one for me.

<u>Can You See</u>

Can you see that you and I are meant to be?

Like the birds and the bees

Like bears and honey

Like the stars and the moon

Like day and night

Like milk and chocolate

Like PB and J

Like you and me.

<u>Can You See</u>

Can you see that I need you?

That you are all that I am & more

That without you I'm just

A lonely soul that trying find true love

That you what complete me

What make me laugh?

What make me smile?

What make me?

<u>Can't Do This</u>

I can't do this just friend thing anymore
I got to be with you

Got to be your man

Got to be the one that put a smile on your face

Got to be your black night

Got to be the one that give you goosebumps
When I'm around you

Got to be the one you can't live without

Got to be the one you always have on your mind

Got to be the one for you.

<u>Days & Nights</u>

Days & nights thinking about you

Thinking about how lucky I am to have you

How I thank The Most High that I found you

How I never thought I would ever feel

So love

So special

So unbelievable happy

How you are everything I pray for

Everything I need & want

How you mean the world to me.

<u>Didn't Realize</u>

Didn't realize what I had till it was gone

Now just sitting here wondering what could have been

What could have been the best thing to?
Happen to me

What could have been my soulmate?

What could have been my guardian angel?

What could have been my golden star?

What could have been my diamonding in the rough?

What could have been something amazing?

<u>Does He</u>

Does he love you like I do?

Does he put you first like I do?

Does he take care of you like I do?

Does he treasure you like I do?

Does he buy you the finest things like I do?

Does he treat you like a queen like I do?

Does he?

<u>Don't Judge Me</u>

Don't judge me by your pass relationship

Don't judge me by how other guys treated you in the pass

*Don't judge me by your painful discovery that you were
with boys not a man*

Instead

Judge me by the way I make you feel

Judge me by what your heart says

Judge me by the days we spent together

Judge me by the way I hold you when you scare

Judge me by the way I treat you as my gold star

Judge me by the love we share

Judge me by the way I am with you.

<u>Don't Judge Me</u>

Don't judge me by the way I talk

The way I walk

The way I think

The way I dress

Or the way I maybe look to you

Cause if you just stop and get to know me

You will find a good friend

A cool person to hang out with

It like they say never judge a book by it covers

So never judge a person by the way they look.

<u>Everything Is Messed Up</u>

Everything is messed up
Money making is more important than life
Selling our soul for the high life
For the fame and power
Not thinking about the next man all about me and just me
Not caring about our brothers & sisters and the
Suffering they go through everyday
Not seeing the aftermath of our obsessing of gaining power
Not realizing that it way more to life than power & fame.

<u>Fond Memories</u>

*I know that it's as been a long time we haven't seen each
other
But I'm still with you.*

*It's like the memories we have will always keep us from
forgetting each other*

It's kind of weird

But at the same time cool

*In fact I was thinking about the way you use to make me
laugh*

The way you use to make me feel good about my self

The way you use to pushed me to do better

The way you gave me your love, wisdom and blessing

And I thank you for all that you are to me.

<u>Have You Ever</u>

Have you ever falling for someone?

That she the only thing you got on your mind

That you can't eat or sleep without her

That you could picture yourself married her

And starting a family with her

That she makes you believe in love

That she perfect in every way

That she can't be replace

That she makes you feel whole

That she makes you a one-woman man

That she all you want & need.

<u>Have You Ever</u>

Have you ever thought that you will feel
Or experience true love

The kind of love that is pure like snow

The kind of love that will never end or go away

I mean unconditional love

The kind of love that speak to your soul

The kind of love that warm your heart

The kind of love that leave you feeling on cloud 9 all day.

<u>He The One</u>

He the one you love

The one you care about

The one you lie for

The one you plan to have kids with

But he treats you like shit

The one you willing to die for

The one you want to spend your entire life with

The one you slave for

But he treats you like shit

When will you going see that he not

The one for you.

<u>He Will Never</u>

He will never love you like I would

He will never appreciate you like I would

He will never understand you like I would

He will never treat you like the queen that you are
Like I would

He will never go through fire for you like I would

He will never see you as that special rose like I would

He will never be the kind of bf you deserve.

<u>How Can I</u>

How can I show you that I love you?

How can I bring joy to your broken heart?

How can I be your teddy bear that you adore?

How can I be your chocolate Sunday?

How can I be the one you led on?

The one you put your faith in

The one you give the key to your soul

The one that makes you smile

The one that makes you laugh

The one that makes you feel oh my God

The one that make you happy

How can I be the one for you?

<u>How Can Love Be</u>

How can love be so painful?

So heartless

So self-center

So disrespectful

So dishonest

So not understanding

How can love be this way?

How Can We Be

How can we be when you don't know?

How to be faithful

When you can't open to me

When you don't believe that I love you

That I would do anything to see you happy

That I wouldn't do anything to hurt you

That I will be by your side to the end

When you can't call me bae

When you don't show me you want to be my girl.

How Can You Say

How can you say I love you when you don't?

How can you say I will be there
when you are nowhere to be found?

How can you say I care about you
when you only care about yourself?

How can you say I understand what you are going through
when you haven't been in my shoes?

How can you say I'm different from the others
when you are just like the others?

How can you say I'm your friend
when you're just in it for the money?

How can you?

<u>How Could You</u>

How could you stab me in back?

How could you take my heart and tear it into pieces

When I love you

When I would do anything for you

When I would of giving you the world

When I open my heart to you

When I treated you like a queen

When I would of giving my life for you

When I thought we had something special

Something worth holding on to

I guess I was wrong.

<u>I Am</u>

I am stronger than a bull

Faster than a cheetah

Braver than an Eagle

Smarter than a fox

Nuttier than a monkey

Smoother than a snake

Hipper than a kangaroo

I am who I am.

I Don't Get It

I don't get you

You said you want out

But you still with him

I don't know why I believe you

Believing that you want someone that at least respect you

Someone that won't try to hurt you to feel good

Someone that will be faithful

Someone that will give you the world

Someone that in it to the end

Someone that will spend his days making you happy
And taking care of

Someone that will treat you empress

Someone like me.

<u>I Don't Know</u>

I don't know how long you going to push me away

I don't know what happen in the pass

But I do know that now you have someone

That want to be with you

That wants to change your sadness to happiness

That really wants to show you that you are worth more
than gold

That you are precious as a ruby

That you are bright like the morning star

That you are gorgeous as the Garden of Eden

That you are one of a kind

And deserve to be treated like a goddess that you are.

I Don't Want To Be

I don't want to be like those dudes that hurt you

That just leaves you

That plays with your emotion

That uses you for sex

That disrespects you

That treats you like shit when you are a queen

That says one thing and means another thing

I just don't want to be.

<u>I Finally Realized</u>

I finally realized that it was you that made me ecstatic

You made me believe in myself

You made me see there is more to life than what I thought

You made me experience something amazing

Now that I lost you, it's like I'm in this matrix and

Nothing seems to make sense

I feel empty inside
And nothing can fly
Or take the pain away

I don't even know if I can make it without you

I need you more than ever before

I miss you more with every passing day

Please return to me.

<u>I Guess</u>

I guess I was wrong to trust you

To let you in my life

To give you all that I have

To show you how true love feel like

To be honest with you

When you weren't with me

To be there for you when no one else was

To be a sucker to your lies

Should have known that fairy tale aren't real.

<u>I Have</u>

I have told you how I feel about you

And you still act like you don't feel the same way
Just want to know why?

Why are you acting hard to get?

Why can't you trust your heart?
And be with me

Why can't you believe that we are meant for each other?

That we have so much in common

That no one will be perfect for u like I am

So why you are being stock up

You know one thing I have learn is that if you don't try or

Put yourself out there you will miss out on a blessing or

Something that you have spent your hold life look for go by

Please don't let us lose something special.

<u>I Have Given Up</u>

I have given up on falling in love

And finding that person that complete me

That will make me happy for rest of my days

That love me the why I love them

That person that will hold me down to the end

But I met you

And I know I found my joy

My light house

My superwoman

My everything.

<u>I Just Want</u>

I just want to go to a place where I can live free to love who
I want
Where I don't have to worry about being killed because
Of my skin color or what I believe in
Where being different is celebrated
Where kindness isn't looked at as weakness
Where greed and hate don't exist
Where violence is never the first option
Where hunger & disease is a thing of the past
Where peace & love for all is the norm
Where imagination and discovery never die out
I just want to go to a place where I can live free.

I Know

I know it is hard to trust me right now

When all your life you been use & mistreated

By other dudes that you thought was the one

The one that would take your pain a way

The one that would sweep you off your feet

The one that would do anything to see you smile

The one that would give you the world

The one that would treat you like empress that you are

The one that would love you like you should be love

If you trust me I can be the one for you.

<u>I Know</u>

I know when you look at me

You see a monster worth being killed in cold blood

Worth being treated less than an animal

Worth being locked up and put in a cage

Worth being call a thug

A gangster

A hoodlum

Worth being hooked to your poison

That you fill my community with

Worth being denied the right to life & pursuit of happiness

Worth being denied the right to be treated as your equal.

<u>I love The Way You Are</u>

The way your smile always put a smile on my face

The way you make this cute face when you make a point

The way you try to see the good in people

The way you laugh at my corny jokes

The way you see through all my faults

The way you give your all to what you believe in

The way you not scare to speak your mind

The way you can make someone feel special when they feel like shit

The way you know how to please me

The way you can be overprotective sometime

The way you keep me grounded

I love everything about you that make you
You.

<u>I Need A Girl</u>

I need a girl that gets me

A girl that can see pass my faults

A girl that can be my strength when I'm weak

A girl that can heal my wounded soul

A girl that fight for what she believes in

A girl that can throw down in the kitchen

A girl that can make me laugh when I'm down

A girl that can bring the best out of me

A girl that can make me believe in love again

A girl like you.

I Need Someone

I need someone that I can relate to

Someone I can put my trust in

Someone that will be there no matter what

Someone that can accept me for who I am

Someone that hold me when I'm scare

Someone that make some good chicken noodle soup

Someone that can give me advice when I need it

Someone with an open heart

Someone like you.

<u>I Need You</u>

I need you to be honest with me

And tell me how you feel about me

Tell me it not only me that feeling you

Tell me that you are feeling we should be together

That we should see if we can be more

If we could be right for each other

If we could be like Adam & Eve

If we could last

I think we owe it to our self to find out.

I Never Knew

I never knew how to tell you that I want to be more than a friend

That I want to be the center part of your soul

That I want to be your air

I want to be the foundation you build your trust

I want to be your shade of comfort

I want to be your guardian light

I want to be fountain of love & happiness

I want to be your ever thing.

<u>I Promise</u>

I promise to love you

To protected you

To be faithful to you

To be honest with you always

To be there through the good & bad

To be your best friend

To be understand to your needs

To be your partner

You're all in all.

<u>I Remember</u>

I remember when you love me

When you put up with me

When I needed a friend to talk to you were always there

When I was sad and down you always tried to make me laugh

When I didn't believe in myself you always believe in me

You saw that I was someone special and unique

You always told me to never give in or give up to always be strong

When you told me that you would always be my number one friend

And you would always be there
But where are you now?
When I need you

When I need your advice and your help

When I need you to say
"keep on going
You can make it."

<u>I Think</u>

I think am in love with you

In love with your smile

With your laughter

With your light brown eyes

With your kinky hair

With your baby soft skin

With your sexy mind

With your freaky ways

I'm just in love with you.

<u>I Thought</u>

I thought you were my dog

My boy but I guess I was wrong

I guess you had to mess with her

You just had to have her to your self

You had to say fuck my best friend this bitch is mine

You knew what she meant to me

You knew she was the one I really love

The one I would have died for

The one I was hoping to spend my life with

You knew that she was my heart

My soul
My sunshine
My joy
My angel

You knew man but still had to go for it
Why, man, why?

<u>I Want</u>

I want to hold you

To kiss you

To make you smile

To make you laugh

To make you have me on your mind always

To make you know that you the most gorgeous girl in the
world to me

To make you know that no one can take your place in my
heart

To make you know how true love feel like

To make you know that I got you no matter what

I will always be by your side.

<u>I Want To Be</u>

I want to be your Romeo

Your sunshine

Your black night

Your partner in crime

Your rock you led on

Your shooting star that make all your wish
Come true

The key to your heart

You're everything?

<u>I Want To Be Free</u>

I want to be free like the bird in the sky

Like the deer in the woods

Like the whale in the ocean

Like the fox in forest

Like the lion in the jungle

Like the turtle in the sea

Like the frog in the pone

Like the fish in the lake

I just want to be free.

<u>I Want To Know</u>

I want to know if you like me more than a friend

If you think about me as much I think about you

If you fantasize about us being together forever

If your heart beats faster when I'm around you

If you believe in us as I do

Could I be your Mr. Right?

<u>I Want You</u>

I want you so badly

That I don't know what to do with myself

That you make me feel sky high

That you make me believe there's somebody
out there for me

That you bring pleasure to my life

That you give my soul tranquility

That you brighten days

That I'm so lucky to have u.

<u>I Want You To Know</u>

I want you to know I think about you every day

That I can't stop thing about

How your smile brightens my day

How your laughter heals my soul

How your touch takes my pain away

How your beauty is hypnotizing

How your voice is music to my ears

How your mind is the sexiest thing about you

How your personality brings out the best out of me

How you just amazing.

<u>I Will Be There</u>

I will be there to holed you

To protected

To love you

To care for you

To treasure you

To turn your sad days to happy ones

To be yours and only yours.

I Wish

I wish I could be with her

To hold her

To kiss her

To make her know that I'm deeply feeling her

To make her know that she everything

I want in women

To make her laugh

To make her smile from ear to ear

To make her know that she can count on me

*To make her know that she the most beautiful girl I
ever seen*

To make her know that she the queen to my soul

To make her know that she the only girl for me.

<u>If</u>

If you give me a chance

You will see that I'm not like the other dude you've been with

I'm not going to hurt you

I'm not going to lie to you

I'm not going to leave you

I'm not going to use you or mistreat you

If you give me a chance you will see that

*I'm nothing like the other dude
You been with.*

<u>If I Only</u>

If I only stop & think about

What you mean to me

You will still be mines

Now I'm just regretting letting you go

Letting you walk out of my life

Letting you be with another guy

Letting others come between us

Letting their lies & jealous destroy the love we had

Now the only things I have are memories

Memories of the good time we had.

<u>I'm Done</u>

I'm done with all the lies.

Done with all the late nights wondering if you alright

Done with u clubbing hang out till morning

Done with sleeping a lone

Done with all the fighting and arguing

Done with all the promises that things will change

I'm done with you.

<u>I'm So Lucky</u>

I'm so lucky to have someone
Like you in my life

I was stupid to think about messing
Up what we have

I'm glad that you

Are giving me a second chance

To redeem myself and

I promise that I won't

Do anything to hurt you again

That I won't take you for granted

That I will be more supportive

That I will be up front with you

I hope I will be lucky enough

To always have you in my life.

<u>I'm Trying</u>

I'm trying to get you to notice me

To get you to know the real me

To get you to trust me

To let me in your heart

To get you to feel me the way I'm feeling you

To get you to be my girl

My hot fudge

My whip creams

My caramel apple

My banana split

To get you to be mine.

<u>Is This Love</u>

Is this really love?

The kind of love I dream about

The kind of love I pray for

The kind of love I waited all my life for

The kind of love I see in fairytale

The kinds of love God have for all of us

The kind of love that is made in heaven

Is this true love?

<u>Is This Real</u>

Is this real

Cause I been here before

Thinking it real

But finding out it was just a delusion
Making me believe

I got something precious

Something worth fighting for

Something that would last forever

Something that would have given a kid like me

Hoping that I found true love

But again it wasn't.

<u>It's Funny</u>

It's funny how you played me

How you made me fall for you

How made me think you were
The one for me

The girl of my dreams

The one I would grow old with

The one that would hold me down
No matter what

The one that saw something special in
What we had

The one that believe in us

But I guess I was wrong.

<u>It Seems</u>

It seems like they are jealous of me

Jealous of the way I talk elegantly

The way I walk with purpose

The way I always have a smile on my face

The way I always look successful

The way I always shining like a star

The way I dance side to side

The way I carry myself with respect

They are just jealous of the way I am.

<u>Just Want</u>

Just want to be a part of your life

To be your best friend that you confide in

To be your rock when you weak

To be your shooting star that

Make your dream come true

To be your fortress of love

To be your prince charming

To be your light house

In this dark world

To be yours.

<u>Just Want To Know</u>

Just want to know how come you willing to give

'Mr. Perfect' a chance and not me

When I treat you better than he does?

When I give my all to you

When I'm always honest and up front with you

When I'm always there for you no matter what

When I know everything about you

How you like orange soda like I do

How your favorite color is blue & Red

How you and brother really close

Since your dad pass a way

How you really miss him

How you like making people laugh

How you this amazing girl

That I'm lucky to call my best friend

When he doesn't love you, like I do.

<u>Last Night</u>

Last night I was sitting on my step and crying

Crying my heart out to you asking you to forgive me

Asking you to give me a second chance to prove to you that I will never hurt you again

That I will devote my life to you

That I will be there when you need me

That I will be your personal salve

That I will do anything to have you back with me.

<u>Lonely Night</u>

Lonely night just thinking about you

Thinking about how I fucked up

How I hurt you

How I miss you

How I need you

How I pushed away the only one that loved me

The only one that cared a whole lot about me

How I wish I can take back all the mean things I said and did.

<u>Love Is</u>

Love is me & you

Being there for one other

Being true with one other

Being one other foundation

Caring for one other

Supporting one other

Understanding one other

Forgiving one other

Respecting one other

That what love is.

<u>Many Nights</u>

Many nights of feeling lonely

Many nights of regrets

Many nights fill with hate

Many nights of telling lies

Many nights of feeling abandoned

Many nights of feeling not wanting to go on

Many nights of seeing no end to my pain.

<u>My Coach</u>

My Coach Mr. Butler

What can I say?

Well for one

Thank you for your support

And

Thank you for being a good role model for me

Thank you for listening

Thank you for giving me a chance

Thank you for inspiring me to do my best

And Most of All

THANK YOU FOR BEING YOU!

<u>Nothing More</u>

It's nothing more that I can say or do

For you to be mine

For you to give me a chance to show you

How you make me feel

How I thank God for sending me one of his Angles

To heal my wounded soul

To save me from my evil ways

To guide me through the storms of life

To be my light in this dark world

To be my forever star

To be my one and only girl.

<u>Only</u>

Only your love can fill the emptiness inside me

Only your smile can bring joy to my soul

Only your touch can heal my loneliness

Only your laugher can put a smile on my face

Only your kiss can give me the shiver

Only your beauty can hypnotize me

Only your.

<u>Only You</u>

Only you can make my heart beat faster

Only you can make me lost for words

Only you can make me laugh out the blue

Only you can make me feel brand new

Only you can give me butterflies

Only you can make my sad days into happy ones

Only you can bring out the best out of me

Only you can see pass my bull shit

Only you can take my loneliness away

Only you can accept me for who I am

Only you can.

<u>Poems</u>

Poems that make you laugh

Poems that make you cry

Poems that make you smile

Poems that make you sad

Poems that empower you

Poems that entertain you

Poems that educate you

Poems that express the inner you.

Say

Say that you want me

Say that you need me

Say that you love me

Say that you will never leave me

Say that you can't live without me

Say that I'm your heart

Your sunshine

Your summer rains

Say that I'm yours forever.

<u>Seeing How You Are</u>

Seeing how things are

Getting school to the games you play

The lies you tell

The heartbreak you cause

The emptiness you leave

The backstabbing you do

The evil you spread

Seeing the truth of your deceiving ways.

<u>She Doesn't Want</u>

She doesn't want to be with me

She wants to be with some jerk

Some jerk that doesn't love her

Some jerk that hits her to feel good about himself

Some jerk that just fucks and leaves her

Some jerk that's only around when it's beneficial to him

Nobody should be with a jerk like him

Especially her.

<u>She Found</u>

She found someone else to love her
Someone to treat her as the Goddess that she is
Someone to be there for her through the good and the bad
Someone that put her first
Some one that treasures her
Someone that tell her that she the most beautiful girl in the
world
Someone that doesn't take her for granted
Someone that show her the good life
Someone that satisfies all her needs
Someone that isn't you.

<u>Tell Me</u>

Tell me how I can be yours

When you don't trust me

When you can't say I love you

When you want me to be with other girls?

When you make me feel that don't want to be with me

When every time I call you seem too busy to talk to me

When you can't let me in your heart

When it seems best to just leave you lone?

<u>Thank You Mom</u>

The one who gave me life
The one that took care of me when I was little
The one who always told me, 'love'
The one I could always go to when I needed comfort
The one who will always be my best friend
The one who is always there for me
The one who is always encourages me
The one that always love me

No matter what I do
Or
Say

For all these reasons
I want to say

Thank Mom

Thank you for loving me
Thank you for taking care of me
Thank you for being there when I needed you the most
Thank you for always believe in me
Thank you for pushing me to go on to achieve my dreams
Thanks Mom.

That Girl

That girl that take my breath away

That girl that gives me butterflies

That girl that quench my desire for love

That girl that sees passes all my faults

That girl that more precious than gold

More gorgeous than Niagara Falls

More exotic than a great white shark

More fun than playing video games

That girl for me.

<u>The Kind Of Girl</u>

The kind of girl you fantasize about

The kind of girl that accepts you for you

The kind of girl you waited your whole life for

The kind of girl that speaks to your soul

The kind of girl that you would do anything for

The kinds of girl that makes you want to settle down
And start a family with

The kind of girl that you would take home to meet
your mom

The kind of girl you would want as your wife

The kind of girl that respects her body

The kind of girl that is not scared to speak her mind

The kind of girl that would hold you down

The kind of girl that fights for what she want

The kind of girl that puts God before everything
The kind of girl that was made for you.

<u>The Man</u>

The soul man

The hip hop man

The high paid man

The don't take any shit man

The hardworking man

The middle class man

The cool man

The ladies kind of man

The down to earth man

The God-fearing man

The man.

<u>The One</u>

The one you adore

The one you would do anything for

The one you would die for

The one that you put your faith in

The one that make you smile from ear to ear

The one that you can't stop think about

The one that make you laugh out of the blue

The one that you could see starting a family with

The one that make you feel special inside and out

The one for you.

<u>The Only One</u>

The only one I desire

The only one I admire

The only one I ache for

The only one I'd die for

The only one I'm willing to go thought hell fire for

The only one I'd give my heart to

The only one I willing to wait for

The only one I want to see walking to the altar

The only one I need & want

The only one for me.

They Only See

They only see me as a drug dealer

They only see me as a killer

They only see me as a rapist

They only see me as a robber

They only see me as a gangster

They only see me as a thug

They only see me as a hustler

They only see what they want to see cause

They can't see that I'm a lawyer

A doctor

A carpenter

An engineer

A teacher

An actor

They only see what they want to see.

<u>Thinking About You</u>

Think about you

Wondering if I made a mistake of letting you go

Cause it driving me crazy not having you next to me

Not being able to kiss you when I want

Not being able to wake up to your beautiful smile

Not being able to play fight like we use to

Or do the other things that we were good at

Not being able to watch our favorite videos

Not being able to go to Paris together

Just not being able to be with you.

<u>Thought We Had</u>

Thought we had something special

Something that's worth hold on to

Something that's worth dying for

Something that's worth killing for

Something that can't be broken

Something that's more precious than gold

Something that's purer than fresh snow

Something that was made in the heavens

Something that was perfect.

<u>Through Dose Eyes</u>

Through dose eyes I can love again

Through dose eyes I can see again

Through dose eyes can feel again

Through dose eyes I can smile again

Through dose eyes I can laugh again

Through dose eyes I can hope again

Through dose eyes I can fly again

Through dose eyes I can be free again.

<u>To Be Honest</u>

To be honest I just wanted to be with you
Cause of what they say about you

I wasn't supposed to fall for you
But I have & now

The only thing I can think about is

Being with you

Being your best friend

Your prince Charmin

Your diamond that you cherish deeply

Your foundation you build your trust on

Your fountain of love

Your everything.

<u>Too Late</u>

Too late to say I'm sorry

For all the wrong I did

For the hell I put you through

For the lies I told

For the heartache I cause

For not being faithful enough

For not being there when you needed me

For not appreciating you

For not trusting you with my heart

For letting others come between what we had

For not being the man you deserve.

<u>What Can I Say</u>

What can I say to get you back?

For you to forgive me

For you to trust me again

For you to love me the way you use to

For you to let me back into your heart

For you to be my junebug

For you to be mine once more.

<u>What Happened</u>

What happened to us?

What happened to the love we had?

To all the fun times together

To the late-night walks on the beach

To the moon light dinners

To staying up till sun rise

To the future we plan

To being together forever

What happened?

<u>What Is</u>

What are days without nights

Pb without J

Honey without the bees

Chocolate without milk

A song without words

A book without pages

Joy without sadness

Love without pain

What is me without you?

<u>What Is Love</u>

Love is caring

Love is kind

Love is cheerful

Love is forgiving

Love is understanding

Love is compassion

Love is supporting

Love is pure

Love is true

Love is you and me.

<u>What Makes You Think</u>

What makes you think that you can treat me like shit?

That you can just use my feeling for your amusement

For you to break my Heart over and over again

For you to act like you doing me a favor

By being with me

For you to keep on bring up my mistake to hurt me.

For you to tell your friends I'm no good deadbeat.

For you to walk out without saying anything

Like goodbye or me and you are done with

For you to blame me for everything that wrong in your life

For you to be a bitch to me.

<u>What Will It Take</u>

What will it take to see the end of human suffering?

What will it take to see a black person or woman be the
president of the U.S

What will it take to see the end to all kind of slavery?

What will it take to see the end of police brutality?

What will it take to see fathers being role model for their
kids?

What will it take to see more young man in college then in
prison?

What will it take to see more youth helping each other than
killing each other?

What will it take to find the cure for AIDS/HIV and other deadly disease?

What will it take to see the end of racism and the injustice it causes?

What will it take?

<u>When</u>

When will the useless killing by cops stop?
When will the violence that played throughout our youth
stop?
When will the drugs that flowed through our communities'
end?
When will the hate that keeps us from being friends end?
When will the greed that people have go?
When will all the homeless find their own homes?
When will the injustices be erased?
When will our world be a better place?
When?

<u>When Will You</u>

When will you stop going out with these boys and go out with a real man?

A man that will respect you and your body

A man that will treat you like a Godless

A man that will support you

A man that will buy you the finest things

A man that will listen to you

A man that will cater to all your needs

A man that will put you before his self

A man that will put is life on the line for you

A man like me.

<u>Who Are You</u>

Who are you that take my breath away?

Who are you that open my eyes to see true beautify?

Who are you that make my soul feel so high?

Who are you that give me a reason to live?

A reason to love

A reason to shine

A reason to share my life with you.

<u>Why</u>

Why do I feel happy when I see you?

Why do I get tongue tied when I talk to you?

Why does my heart beat faster when I'm around you?

Why does my soul sing when I'm thinking about you?

Why do I get nervous when you kiss me?

Why do I get scared of mess up what we have?

Why do I do the stuff that I do?

<u>Why Can't I</u>

Why can't I be your man?

When I would do anything to see you smile

When I would give you all I have and more

When I would be there for you doing your ups & down

When I would put you before everything I do

When I would treat you like a godless

When I would go through fire to be with you

When I would give my life up for you

When I would love you like no one else could love you

Why can't we be?

<u>Why Did I</u>

Why did I let you go?

Why did I let the opinion of others come between us?

Why didn't I trust in what we had?

Why did I act like I didn't need you?

Act like you weren't the best thing in my life

Why did I always break my promise to you?

Why did I put other bitches before you?

Why did I made you second guess if I love you?

If I wanted to be with you

Why did I?

<u>Why Do I Care</u>

Why do I care so much about you?
When you don't

Why do I see that you are worth more than you think?

Why do I think you deserve some unique?

Someone you can count on

Someone that respect you

Someone that think your mind and body are sexy

Someone that would treat you like a queen

Someone that would love you like on one else

Someone like me.

<u>Why Do You</u>

Why do you go out with boys?

That cause you pain

That disrespect you

That don't have any kind of love for you

That treat you like shit

That just use you for your body

Why do you put up with it?

<u>Why Do You</u>

Why do you hide your feeling from me?
By playing these games

When I know that you like me

Cause of the way you look at me

The way you talk to me

The way you laugh at my corny jokes

The way you always want to be around me

And by the way you say you do

So why don't you act on those feeling and be with me

Do you like seeing me in pain?

<u>Why You Hate Me</u>

Why do you hate me?

Is it cause I'm smarter than you?

Faster than you

Better looking than you

Get paid way more than you

Got more girls than you

Stronger than you

Drive a nicer car than you

What is it?

<u>Will You Be</u>

Will you be my sunshine on a rainy day?

Will you be my bridge over trouble waters?

Will you be the apple of my eye?

The key to my heart?

The queen of my soul?

Will you be my special rose?

My lost treasure that I cherries deeply

Will you be mine?

<u>Wondering</u>

Wondering why I let her go

Why I treated her badly

Why I push her into another guy arms

Why I made her cry

Why I made her feel less than perfect
When she's amazing

Why did I put my boys before her?

Why I let them disrespect her way they did

Why?

<u>You Are</u>

You are my heart

My soul

My life

My joy

My angel that I adore

My bright golden star

My diamond that I treasure deeply

My guardian light

My tower of comfort

You are all that I am and more

You are the world to me.

You Are Mine

You are mine & I am yours
To love

To treasure

To protected

To comfort

To be there

To the end of time

To be yours and only.

<u>You Lied</u>

I thought you said I was the only one for you

That I make your days brighter

That you can't live without me

That I'm the best person in your life

That we are meant for each other

That we will spend the rest of our days together

I guess all that was lies

Lies for me to hear from you

Lies that can rip my heart out

Lies that can tear it into little pieces

Lies that show me you are not for me

I want someone real and true

I don't want someone who lies.

<u>You Say</u>

You say that you love me

But you don't know what love really is

Because if you did you will know

Love don't see to make your life hell

Love don't lie to you

Love don't talk about you behind your back

Love don't bail on you when you need it the most

Love don't just use you when it's beneficial

Love don't kick you when you down

Love don't make you feel worthless

Love is just not you.

<u>You So</u>

You so want to be Ms. Popular

That you can't see yourself going out
With a nerd

Who would treat you like a goddess?

That would move mountain to be with you

That would put you above everything in is life

That would give you the world

That would do everything & anything to make sure
You are happy

That would basically worship you

But you want to be Mrs. Popular.

<u>You Think</u>

You think that you can break me

That you can bring me down

In the pits of bitterness & hate

That by calling me names & treating me likes shit

You will stop me from achieving my goals

Stop me from being the star I'm destined to be

That you can make me give up on my dreams.

<u>You Were</u>

You were my best pal

The one I could always talk to

The one I always looked up to

The one that always made me laugh

The one that always had my back

The one that always got through to me

The one that always pushed me to be my best

Now that you gone

It's like nothing makes sense

It's like I 'm alone

It's like I lost a part of me that's gone forever.